CONTENTS

C000001194

ACKNOWLEDGEMENTS

My thanks go to the many people who have made possible the creation of *15-Minute STEM*. Thanks to the fantastic team at Crown House Publishing for sharing my enthusiasm for STEM education and for their guidance throughout the process.

Thanks also to Jane Hewitt for bringing the activities to life with her beautiful photographs, and to the school communities – of Darton Primary and Worsbrough Common Primary – who feature in those photos. The book is filled with images of excited, happy children, and this never fails to make me smile as I flick through its pages.

A final thank you goes to my family for always being there to offer a listening ear or a word of encouragement when needed, and to my husband Edmund. Time and time again I have been grateful for his scientific expertise and insight, which has helped me to develop my ideas into the finished product that you see before you today.

INTRODUCTION: THE CASE FOR 15-MINUTE STEM

STEM stands for science, technology, engineering and mathematics. These disciplines have an impact that can be seen in all aspects of our lives. From construction to space exploration, from caring for our environment to the digital revolution; the demand for STEM skills is massive and is only set to grow.

STEM education is a cross-discipline approach to teaching these interrelated subjects, with problem solving at its heart. Great STEM education works through activities with real-world applications, helping children to understand how their learning is relevant and how they could use it in the future. It is an important tool in breaking down stereotypes and encouraging more children to pursue STEM careers. There is a notable under-representation of women and people from ethnic minority backgrounds in STEM careers, so it is important that all children can realise their own capabilities first-hand.

But then again, if you've picked up this book, the chances are you already know all of that. Most teachers and parents recognise STEM to be an important priority area for modern education. However, you may be looking for answers to one or all of the following questions:

How do I fit STEM education into my day?

What kind of STEM activities should I be exploring?

How can I deliver STEM education when I'm not an expert myself?

Is STEM education just for the classroom?

This book is intended to reassure you that you don't need to be an expert to deliver high-quality STEM education. It contains 40 quick, easy-to-resource STEM activities for primary school teachers, and is also ideal for parents to use at home with their children.

How do I fit STEM education into my day?

15-minute STEM activities really do take just 15 minutes

Each activity has been tested to ensure that it can be delivered quickly. This means that with minimal preparation you can slot a 15-minute STEM activity into those spare moments in an otherwise busy day. Of course, it is up to you how much time you spend preparing the children and discussing their findings afterwards.

15-minute STEM is easy to resource

Many of the activities in this book can be resourced from everyday materials found at home or in the classroom, allowing you to deliver them at short notice. Phew! The 'You will need' boxes list the resources you will need to complete each activity once. You will need a set of resources for each child or group undertaking the activity.

It doesn't need to match the curriculum

That's the charm of these 15-minute activities. They can be presented independently of other learning, giving you greater flexibility to slot them in as stand-alone projects. You will find that the children naturally draw upon a range of prior knowledge to complete each activity.

What kind of STEM activities should I be exploring?

STEM activities should make real-world connections

In my experience, children respond best to activities with obvious real-world relevance. Therefore, each activity starts with a question they might ask themselves. It's then up to the children to investigate! I've also linked each activity to STEM careers that engage with conceptually similar tasks, a glossary of which is included at the back of the book. Research shows that the perceptions children have about certain jobs and careers are formed at a young age and that gender stereotyping exists from the age of 7.[1] By introducing children to relevant STEM careers we can challenge these early perceptions and stereotypes and widen their career aspirations.

How can I deliver STEM education when I'm not an expert myself?

Follow the explanation of the learning

Each activity is written as a script that can be delivered directly to children. A helpful 'What are we learning?' box accompanies each activity, which outlines the key learning points. These explanations are targeted towards the primary school age range, equipping you with the key facts you'll need in order to summarise the task.

Less structure, more action

I've kept the activity instructions on the lighter side, and would encourage you to be hands-off with the children. Instead of outlining exactly what the task entails, start with the question, expose the children to the resources and allow them to lead the exploration – supporting them when needed with the step-by-step instructions.

---

1   See Nick Chambers, Elnaz T. Kashefpakdel, Jordan Rehill and Christian Percy, *Drawing the Future: Exploring the Career Aspirations of Primary School Children from Around the World* (London: Education and Employers, 2018). Available at: https://www.educationandemployers.org/wp-content/uploads/2018/01/DrawingTheFuture.pdf.

Is STEM education just for the classroom?

STEM education is for both teachers and parents

These activities can be done at home, as well as in school. In fact, reinforcing STEM principles across these two settings helps to embed the learning in real-life contexts and fosters an interest in these disciplines from a young age.

15-minute STEM is deliberately adaptable

Each activity can be made suitable for specific age groups within the 5–11 range with a little bit of adaptation. Stick to the basic structure of the activity with younger children, and use the 'Investigate' cues to extend the task with older children. This can also be used to extend the activity beyond 15 minutes, depending on the children's engagement with the task. If a whole class is completing the activity there is plenty of scope to discuss and compare results afterwards. Many of the tasks could also be completed in small groups to encourage collaborative problem solving and teamwork.

Oh, and another thing ...

15-minute STEM develops soft skills

Problem solving, critical thinking, teamwork, communication, confidence, spatial awareness ... the list goes on! These hands-on activities are designed to encourage curiosity and creativity, along with a wide range of other important soft skills, which are crucial to success in STEM and other careers.

Now, let's get started!

HEALTH, SAFETY AND A FEW OTHER BITS

- Some activities come with templates or resources for you to copy (e.g. activity 35, Spinning Helicopters), but you might want to have a go at making your own instead.

- Some of the activities are seasonal. For example, activity 13, Leaf Shape Sorting, works best in the autumn when there are lots of fallen leaves. Save these activities for the right time of year.

- Some of the activities are messy! It's a good idea to try them outside and to make sure that you are wearing suitable clothing. This is indicated at the start of these activities – see the key below.

- Some of the activities need to be returned to throughout the day (e.g. activity 5, Chasing Shadows). Again, this is noted at the start of these activities.

- Some of the activities involve the use of single-use plastics such as drinking straws. Where possible, reuse these plastics for other activities.

Some important guidelines to share with the children:

- When working with warm water, take it from the hot tap rather than a boiling kettle.

- When doing outdoor activities, remember to stay within sight of an adult.

- Take care with sharp objects, such as scissors.

- Never taste any of the products of the experiments.

- Wash your hands after completing each experiment and be careful not to touch your eyes.

- Be respectful of the natural environment, being careful not to disturb it.

- When working with living creatures, such as minibeasts, make sure they are returned to where they are found.

Throughout the book you'll find different icons next to the activities. Here's what they mean:

 You will need to return to these activities later in the day to make observations or collect more results.

 These activities can be done individually.

 These activities can be done inside.

 These activities are also suitable for teams.

 These activities are best done outside.

 Be extra safety-conscious with these activities; adult help or accompaniment may be necessary.

1. AIR-POWERED CAR

How can we power a vehicle using a balloon?

You will need

- A balloon
- Cardboard
- Straws x3
- Wooden dowels x2
- Wheels x4 (e.g. cardboard circles, plastic bottle lids, old CDs)
- Sticky tape
- Scissors
- A measuring tape

Investigate

Now adapt your design to see if you can create an air-powered boat. You will need to use a waterproof material for the base of your boat, such as a sponge or a plastic tray.

What are we learning?

The air escaping from the balloon propels the car in the opposite direction. This is an example of Newton's third law of motion (for every action there is an equal and opposite reaction).

The same physics occurs in the launch of space rockets, which burn fuel and eject gases behind them, propelling them upwards. Check out activity 31, Rocket Racers!

How to do it

Note: You will need an adult to pierce the holes for the dowels to go through if you are using plastic bottle lids for your wheels.

1. Create the base of your car from a piece of cardboard.

2. Tape two straws across the base's underside to create the axles (an axle is a rod that connects two wheels).

3. Thread the wooden dowels through the straw axles and attach wheels onto the ends.

4. Tape the third straw to the top of the cardboard base and insert one end into the opening of a balloon, securing with sticky tape.

5. Blow through the other end of the straw to inflate the balloon. Then pinch the end of the straw to keep the air in until you are ready to test it.

6. Place your car on a flat surface and watch it go! Measure the distance that it travels.

Optional: Experiment with using different materials or sizes for the wheels. What works best? Can you think of reasons why? Can you increase the distance that your car travels?

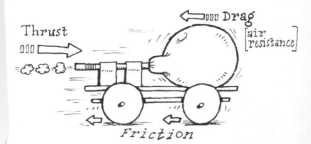

Thrust   Drag [air resistance]   Friction

Mechanical engineer

Physicist

9

2. ARCTIC ENGINEERING

Why are igloos built in a dome shape?

You will need

- Marshmallows
- Cocktail sticks
- A large plate or tray

Investigate

Look for dome and arch shapes in the architecture around you. Can you spot any keystones?

How to do it

1. Begin by creating the circular base of the igloo on your plate or tray. Use the cocktail sticks to secure the marshmallows together closely.

2. As you build up the marshmallow layers, make smaller circles, and curve the sides of the igloo inwards, creating a dome shape. The sides should meet at a single row of marshmallows along the top.

3. Review your design. Is it structurally strong? If you're feeling brave, try building it again without using the cocktail sticks for support.

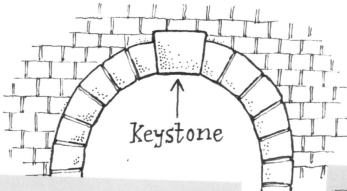

Keystone

What are we learning?

An igloo is a hut built from blocks of compacted snow. Snow is a good material for an igloo because air pockets trapped inside act as an insulator. This means that it prevents heat from escaping.

Igloos are shaped like a dome. This is a structurally strong shape. The final block of snow at the top is usually larger than the ones used to build the walls and is referred to as the keystone. The downward force of its weight holds all the other blocks in place. We can cheat a bit in this activity by using cocktail sticks for support, but in real structures the weight is sufficient to hold the dome together.

Architect

Civil engineer

3. BUBBLE GEOMETRY

How have engineers been inspired by nature?

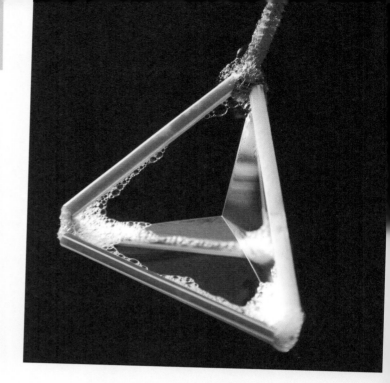

You will need

- Straws
- Pipe cleaners
- Washing-up liquid
- Water
- A bowl
- Glycerine (optional)

How to do it

1. Mix water and a little washing-up liquid together in a bowl to create a bubble solution. You could add a teaspoon of glycerine to help strengthen the bubble solution.

2. Decide on the 3D shapes you will make to dip into your bubble solution. For example, a cube or a pyramid.

3. Cut each straw into quarters. Then thread pipe cleaners into the straws, to start building your 3D shape. Bend the pipe cleaners and use them to join together other straw segments.

4. Once you've made your 3D shape, attach a length of pipe cleaner as a handle.

5. Dip your 3D shape into the bubble mixture and then pull it out to inspect your bubble.

6. Have a good look, then blow your bubble away!

Investigate

Research what other structures have been inspired by nature. Alternatively, find out more about Frei Otto, the German engineer and architect who pioneered the concept of a tensile structure by observing soap bubbles.

What are we learning?

These geometrical bubbles are an example of a tensile structure. Tensile structures are formed when a material is spread out and held in tension between two or more anchors. An example is the dome of London's O2 Arena. These structures can cover large areas with minimal amounts of building material and are very light. Our bubbles stretch between the straws in a similar way.

Architect

Civil engineer

4. CATAPULT CHALLENGE

How can we create a catapult that launches a projectile a long way?

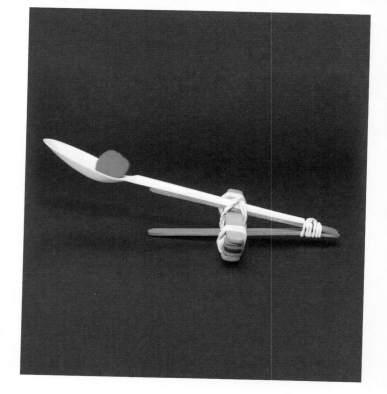

You will need

- Lolly sticks x8
- Rubber bands (lots)
- A plastic spoon
- Soft items to launch as projectiles (e.g. marshmallows or pompoms)
- A measuring tape

Investigate

Research how catapults have been used in the past by ancient and medieval militaries.

What are we learning?

A catapult is a launching device used to fire a projectile (an object) across a distance. Historically they have been used in warfare. When we prepare to fire our catapult, potential energy is stored in the stretched rubber bands. When we release the arm this is converted into kinetic (movement) energy in the spoon which is transferred into the fired projectile, as well as some heat energy in the rubber band.

How to do it

1. Tightly secure six lolly sticks together with a rubber band at each end.

2. Take two additional lolly sticks. These will form the arm and the base of your catapult. Secure them together at one end using a rubber band. Position the lolly stick stack horizontally on the surface in front of you. Then sandwich the stack between the arm and the base, facing vertically. Attach a rubber band around the join in a criss-cross shape.

3. Finally, attach a plastic spoon along the arm of your catapult using more rubber bands.

4. Holding the arm and base's join securely in place, place your projectile on the spoon and bend the arm down with your finger. Release and measure how far the projectile travels!

5. How could you improve your catapult to make your projectile travel further? What's the best launch angle?

Optional: Now adapt your catapult to see how high you can fire your projectile. You could measure height by firing it at a wall and seeing where it hits.

Physicist

Mechanical engineer

5. CHASING SHADOWS

How do shadows change throughout the day?

You will need

- Chalk
- A measuring tape
- A watch or clock
- A clipboard
- Paper
- A pencil

Investigate

A sundial is an instrument that tells the time based on the position of the sun in the sky. Find out more about how sundials work. Can you create your own using natural materials?

What are we learning?

Light travels in a straight line. When we place a solid object, such as a person, in its path, it blocks some of the light, creating a shadow.

As the earth rotates, the relative position of the sun in the sky changes, which changes the length and position of shadows. In the morning your shadow is longer and faces west. By midday the sun is directly overhead, making your shadow short. In the afternoon your shadow grows longer again and faces east.

How to do it

Note: You will need to do this activity on a sunny day. You will need to return to it throughout the day.

1. Begin this activity first thing in the morning. Head outside, stand on a dry, hard surface (e.g. a playground or driveway) and choose a direction in which to face. Get someone to draw around your shadow using chalk.

2. Measure the length and position of your shadow in relation to you (e.g. in front, to the left, or in degrees). Record the time.

3. Decide how regularly you are going to check your shadow throughout the day (e.g. at hourly intervals).

4. Return to check the position of your shadow periodically, standing in the same place each time, with your feet pointing in the same direction. Record your findings.

Optional: Younger children could skip the measurement and draw around each other's shadows in a different colour each time.

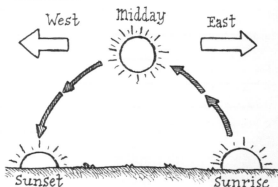

Astronomer

Meteorologist

13

Can be
done inside

Can be done
individually

Be extra safety-
conscious

6. DANCING SALT

How does sound travel?

You will need

- A large bowl
- Cling film
- Salt
- A sound system and speaker
- Food colouring (optional)
- Ingredients with different-sized granules (e.g. rice, granulated sugar and caster sugar)

Investigate

Try placing ingredients with different-sized particles on the cling film (e.g. rice, granulated sugar and caster sugar). Do you notice a difference in the way the different-sized particles vibrate?

How to do it

Note: For best results, place a wireless speaker directly inside the bowl before covering with cling film.

1. Place the cling film tightly over the bowl.

2. Gently pour a small amount of salt onto the centre of the cling film. You could dye the salt with food colouring beforehand so you can see it more clearly.

3. Hold or place the speaker against the bowl. Turn on the sound system and play some music. Move your speaker around at different angles until you can see maximum vibrations in the salt. Take care as you do so to not let the salt particles fall onto the speaker.

4. Observe what happens to the salt as you change the volume. What kind of music makes the salt dance best? What patterns does the salt make?

What are we learning?

The speaker creates sound waves, which are temporary compressions of the air. These disturbances travel through space, transferring energy. The sound waves travel out of the speaker and hit the bowl and cling film, causing them to vibrate. This in turn makes the salt vibrate, or 'dance'. The vibrations cause the salt to move in different ways depending on the frequency (number of sound waves per second) and volume (loudness of each sound wave).

Sound
engineer

Physicist

Best done outside

Can be done individually

Be extra safety-conscious

7. DECODING NATURE'S PATTERNS

What naturally occurring patterns can we find?

You will need

- A camera
- A magnifying glass

Investigate

Architects are often inspired by nature when designing new structures. Research how symmetry, spirals and tessellation are used in architecture.

What are we learning?

The natural world is full of patterns including symmetry, spirals and tessellation. Mathematicians and scientists try to explain these patterns. A pattern is symmetrical when a line can be drawn through it and each side of that line looks exactly the same. A spiral is a curve that winds around a central point. A pattern is said to tessellate when the shapes fit together perfectly with no gaps or overlaps.

How to do it

1. Head outside for a nature walk to look for patterns in nature. Keep your eyes peeled for the following in particular:

   ◎ Symmetry. Examples of this can be found in flowers or on butterflies' wings.

   ◎ Spirals. Examples of this can be found in shells or draining water.

   ◎ Tessellation. Examples of this can be found in tree bark or the patterns of a fish's scales.

2. Use your magnifying glass to take a closer look at each pattern. Then take a photo. Why do you think there are so many examples?

Optional: The Fibonacci sequence is a sequence of numbers in which each number adds up to the two numbers before it: 0, 1, 1, 2, 3, 5, 8, 13, and so on. For older children, take a closer look at the petals on flowers, seed heads or the spiral of a pine cone or a snail's shell. These are all examples of the Fibonacci sequence in nature.

Symmetry *Spiral* *Tessellation*

Mathematician

Naturalist

Best done outside

Can be done individually

Suitable for teams

Be extra safety-conscious

8. DESERT ISLAND RAFTS

How can we create a raft out of natural materials?

You will need

- Sticks
- Twine
- A bowl
- Water
- Leaves (optional)
- Coins (optional)
- Scissors

Investigate

Explore how much weight your raft can carry by adding an additional load to it (e.g. coins). How could you improve your raft to carry more weight?

What are we learning?

A raft is the most basic form of boat design. Rafts were traditionally made of wood because this material is widely available in the natural environment. Wood floats because it is less dense than water (for more on the forces involved see activity 38, Tinfoil Cargo Boats).

How to do it

Note: Children may need assistance to make the sticks a suitable length, and guidance to tie them together.

1. Imagine you were stranded on a desert island. What natural resources could you use to help you escape?

2. Go on a nature walk outside to collect sticks. If needed, snap them down to a suitable length. You may need an adult to help you with this.

3. Select two base sticks. They will go at opposite ends of your raft. The remaining sticks will form the deck of your raft.

4. Position one of your base sticks underneath one of the deck sticks to create an L shape. There should be a slight overlap at the ends of each stick. Then wrap twine around the join in the sticks in a criss-cross shape to secure them together.

5. Repeat this at the opposite end of the deck stick, securing it with twine to the other base stick. Then use another deck stick to join the remaining two corners of the raft.

6. Use your remaining deck sticks to create the main deck of the raft, securing them with twine.

7. Test your raft in a bowl of water. Does it float? If not, how could you improve it?

Optional: Create a decorative mast using a stick and a leaf. How does this affect the balance of your raft?

Sailor

Naval engineer

9. DROPS ON A PENNY

How many drops of water can a penny hold?

You will need

- A penny
- A pipette
- Paper towels
- Water
- A different liquid, e.g. cooking oil, for comparison (optional)

Investigate

Which side of the penny holds water best? Heads or tails? Do we get the same result (number of drops) if we use a different liquid such as cooking oil?

How to do it

1. Make a prediction about how many water drops you think you will be able to fit on a penny. Record your prediction so you can see how accurate it is!

2. Place your penny on top of a paper towel on a flat surface.

3. Fill a pipette with water. Then gently squeeze one water drop at a time onto the centre of the penny. Count the number of drops, recording this using a tally chart.

4. Continue until the water spills over the edge of the penny.

5. How many drops of water did your penny hold? How does this compare to your prediction?

What are we learning?

As we add more drops of water onto the penny we see a dome shape forming. The water molecules are attracted to each other and make a single large drop. At the same time, a property called surface tension tries to minimise the surface area of the water, making the curve shape. This also prevents the water from spilling out. However, as we add more drops, the gravitational pull on the weight of the water eventually becomes more powerful than the surface tension, causing the water to spill.

Chemist

Physicist

Best done
outside

Can be done
individually

Suitable for
teams

10. EGG PARACHUTES

Can we drop an egg from a height without breaking it?

You will need

- An egg
- Junk modelling materials (e.g. card, tissue paper, polystyrene packing)
- A carrier bag or plastic sheeting
- String
- Sticky tape
- Scissors

How to do it

Note: The egg drop should take place outside in case of mess!

1. The challenge is to create a parachute that will safely transport an egg to the ground from a height without it breaking. Begin by building a protective egg holder using your modelling materials.

2. Next, create the parachute using plastic from your carrier bag or sheeting. Once complete, use the string to attach the parachute to the egg holder.

3. Take your design outside, put your egg in the holder and drop it from a height to test it. Make and test other designs. Which was the most successful? Why?

Optional: You could make this more challenging by imposing design limits (e.g. you can only use a maximum of three materials to make the egg holder).

Investigate

Find out about the different materials and shapes used in packaging to protect breakable objects. What works best and why?

What are we learning?

Before we drop the egg it has potential energy, from being lifted up against the pull of gravity. The higher the egg, the more potential energy it has. As the egg falls, this is converted into kinetic (movement) energy. When it hits the ground, this energy has to go somewhere – like into the egg, causing the shell to break!

The parachute can help to slow the speed of the fall, decreasing the kinetic energy and therefore protecting the egg. Protective holders can absorb the kinetic energy on impact, so this doesn't travel into the fragile eggshell.

Aerospace engineer

Physicist

11. FIREWORKS IN A JAR

What happens when we mix fluids of different densities?

You will need

- A clear jar
- Warm water
- Vegetable oil
- Food colouring (in a variety of colours)
- A pipette (optional)
- Other liquids, e.g. honey or milk, for comparison (optional)

How to do it

1. Part-fill your jar with warm water, leaving space at the top.

2. Then add a 2-centimetre layer of vegetable oil. You will notice that the oil floats on top of the water.

3. Place droplets of different shades of food colouring onto the oil layer, either by squeezing them from the bottle or using a pipette. The larger the droplet, the quicker it will sink through the oil layer.

4. Watch as the coloured droplets sink down into the water and mix together, creating fireworks!

Investigate

Now try adding other fluids to your jar, such as honey or milk. How do their densities compare to water and vegetable oil?

What are we learning?

Density is the mass of an object divided by its volume. Put another way, it is the amount of 'stuff' that can fit in a given space. Some materials are very light for their size while others are very heavy. For example, a brick and a sponge might be a similar size but the sponge would be a lot lighter. This is because it is less dense. Oil is less dense than water so it floats to the top of the jar. The food colouring droplets sink into the water because they are denser than the oil. They diffuse in the water (spread out completely), creating what looks like fireworks.

Chemist

Petroleum geologist

19

Return to activity later

Can be done inside

Can be done individually

12. GREEN COINS

How can we make dull coins shiny again?

You will need

- Dull copper coins
- Small bowls (one bowl per liquid used)
- Water
- A range of acidic liquids (e.g. lemon juice, vinegar, cola)
- Salt (optional)

Investigate

Take a walk around your local area to see if you can find examples of copper that has turned green on buildings. Church roofs are often made from copper.

How to do it

Note: You will need to return to this activity throughout the day.

1. Pour a small amount of each liquid into separate bowls and label them.

2. Add a dull copper coin to each bowl.

3. Leave the coins for 10 minutes and then take them out of the bowls to check what they look like. What do you notice?

4. Return each coin to the same bowl and leave them for a longer period of time (e.g. an hour).

5. Remove the coins for a final time and rinse them under the tap. Which liquid was most effective at making them shiny?

Optional: Try the experiment using vinegar again, but this time add a small amount of salt. What happens to the speed of the reaction?

What are we learning?

Each coin is made partly of a metal called copper. Over time, the copper surface reacts with oxygen in the air to form copper oxide, turning the metal dull. When we expose the coins to acidic liquids, such as vinegar or lemon juice, the acid dissolves the copper oxide, making them shiny again. Salt can speed up the rate of this reaction.

We see the same oxidising reaction happening on copper structures – most famously the Statue of Liberty in New York.

Chemist

Architect

Best done outside | Can be done individually | Suitable for teams

13. LEAF SHAPE SORTING

How many differently shaped leaves can we find?

You will need

- A3 leaf shape sorting sheet (see template on page 22)
- A nature book, or the Leafsnap UK app*

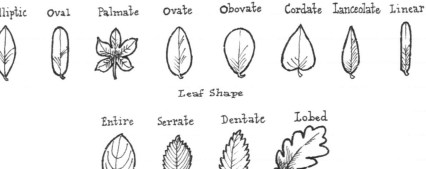

Elliptic   Oval   Palmate   Ovate   Obovate   Cordate   Lanceolate   Linear

Leaf Shape

Entire   Serrate   Dentate   Lobed

Leaf Edges

Investigate

Choose your favourite leaf from your collection and find out what type of tree it comes from. You can use a nature book to identify it, or photograph the leaf against a white background using the Leafsnap UK app, which will identify the species for you.

What are we learning?

The scientific study of trees and leaves is called dendrology. Scientists classify leaves in lots of different ways, including by their shape and how their edges look.

Leaves from the same tree or plant can vary in appearance and size. However, they will always roughly correspond to the same basic shape.

How to do it

Note: Autumn is the best time of year for this activity!

1. Begin by taking a leaf walk to collect a variety of leaves. Remember to only collect leaves that are on the ground.

2. Sort the leaves, using the leaf shape sorting sheet. If you prefer, you can create your own simpler categories for leaf sorting, such as by size or colour.

3. After sorting your leaves, discuss what you have found (e.g. number and variety, different tree types, etc.).

Dendrologist

Botanist

* See http://www.nhm.ac.uk/take-part/identify-nature/leafsnap-uk-app.html.

LEAF SHAPE SORTING SHEET

LEAF SHAPE / ← LEAF EDGES	ENTIRE	SERRATE	DENTATE	LOBED
ELLIPTIC				
OVAL				
PALMATE				
OVATE				
OBOVATE				
CORDATE				
LANCEOLATE				
LINEAR				

Can be done inside

Can be done individually

Suitable for teams

14. LOLLY STICK BRIDGES

What bridge designs are strongest?

You will need

- Lolly sticks
- Glue
- Plasticine
- Strong tape (e.g. masking tape)
- Toy cars
- A measuring tape

Investigate

Research the following types of bridge: beam, suspension, truss and arch. See if you can find a famous example of each type.

What are we learning?

Overlapping and criss-crossing lolly sticks will help to make the base of the bridge stronger. Some shapes are stronger than others. For example, a truss bridge uses triangles to spread out the weight, creating a stronger design than one using squares or rectangles. Using more lolly sticks doesn't necessarily make for a stronger bridge: they also add more weight to the structure!

How to do it

1. Think about the bridges that you have seen. What do they look like? What are they made of? How are they designed?

2. Use lolly sticks to create a bridge that will span a 30-centimetre gap. This could be between two tables or chairs of the same height. You can choose how to attach the lolly sticks together, using the range of adhesive materials on offer. You may want to begin by creating the base of the bridge. Remember that glue will take time to dry, so you won't be able to test it straight away!

3. Once you've finished your design, test the bridge using the toy cars to see how much weight it can hold.

4. Was your bridge successful? If not, how could you improve it? Could a different design hold more toy cars?

Architect

Civil engineer

Can be done inside   Can be done individually

15. MAGIC MILK

How does washing-up liquid make things clean?

You will need

- Whole milk
- Washing-up liquid
- A bowl
- A pipette
- Food colouring
- Cotton buds
- Semi-skimmed milk (optional)

How to do it

1. Pour a layer of milk into a bowl.

2. Use a pipette to squeeze different coloured drops of food colouring onto the surface of the milk. Make sure each drop is placed towards the centre of the bowl.

3. Dip a cotton bud into the washing-up liquid.

4. Place the washing-up liquid coated cotton bud into the centre of the milk and hold it there for approximately 15 seconds.

5. Watch the magic unfold!

6. Explore whether the speed of the reaction and the way the colours disperse changes if you use more washing-up liquid.

Investigate

Try the experiment again, but this time use semi-skimmed milk. Does the reaction change? Why might this be?

What are we learning?

Milk is mostly water, but it also contains vitamins, minerals, proteins and tiny droplets of fat. Washing-up liquid is designed to break down fat. When we add the two together we see a chemical reaction. Liquids such as water and milk have surface tension. This means that the molecules cling together tightly, creating a kind of 'skin' on the surface. When we add washing-up liquid it breaks the surface tension and disrupts the food colouring to create a burst of colour.

Chemist

Colour technician

24

16. MARBLE RUN MAYHEM

What happens to a marble as it moves through a marble run?

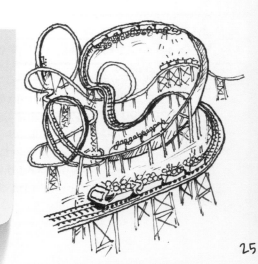

You will need

- Cardboard tubes
- Scissors
- Removable 'magic' tape
- A marble
- A timer (optional)

Investigate

Roller coasters use height to create lots of potential energy. Various forces create different sensations on the riders as they are taken around the track, often at great speed. Find out more about the physics of roller coasters. Which forces are involved?

Physicist

Mechanical engineer

How to do it

1. Locate a suitable flat vertical surface, such as a wall, to build your marble run on.

2. Cut each cardboard tube in half to create the marble run ramps and bumpers. You could vary the length of the tubes to add variety to your marble run.

3. Begin by attaching the first tube at the top of your marble run using removable tape. Position it so it is tilting downwards slightly.

4. Continue to attach cardboard tubes down the length of the marble run. Vary the angles of the tubes to create different speeds of travel.

5. Check your marble run from the top as you go, making sure your marble is able to travel downwards between the runs.

6. Test your marble run. Does it work?

Optional: The challenge is to create a marble run that takes exactly 30 seconds to complete. You may need a lot of tubes!

What are we learning?

Before we release the marble at the start of the run it has potential energy from being lifted to a height. As it rolls along the angled tubes, this converts into kinetic (movement) energy. Gravity is the force pulling the marble to the ground. It would take it straight down if not for the angled runways, which instead guide the marble down and sideways. As the marble rubs against the cardboard tubes it also creates an opposing force called friction. This slows down the marble. Angles are critical to the marble run's success. The greater the angle, the quicker the marble will roll.

Can be
done inside

Can be done
individually

Suitable for
teams

17. MARSHMALLOW CHALLENGE

What is the tallest structure we can make using spaghetti and marshmallows?

You will need

- Spaghetti
- Marshmallows
- A measuring tape
- A timer

Investigate

Find out more about how triangles are used in architecture. Some famous examples you could research are the Eiffel Tower in Paris or the so-called Mathematical Bridge in Cambridge.

How to do it

1. Before you begin to make your tall structure, quickly discuss a building strategy. When ready, start the 15-minute timer – you may need an adult to help keep time for you.

2. Using the marshmallows as joins to dig the spaghetti into, begin construction with a firm foundation for your structure. **Hint:** Double up the spaghetti for extra strength and use triangle shapes in your design.

3. As your structure takes shape, remember to make sure it narrows towards the top.

4. Time is up! Measure your tower to see how tall it is.

Optional: Experiment with different designs and discuss why some are more successful than others.

What are we learning?

A successful tower will probably include triangles in the design. Triangles are inherently rigid. This means that when we apply a force to them they don't change their shape. In contrast, when we apply a force to a shape such as a square, it can be deformed into a parallelogram. Doubling up strands of spaghetti helps to strengthen the structure. Digging the spaghetti deeper into the marshmallow makes a sturdier joint. Civil engineers and architects are often asked to create tall towers and must think carefully about their foundations and shape.

Architect

Civil
engineer

18. MINIBEAST MAPPING

Which habitats do minibeasts like to live in?

You will need

- A magnifying glass
- A yoghurt pot
- A paintbrush
- Paper
- A pencil

Investigate

See if you can create a new habitat to attract minibeasts. This could be a leaf pile, stone pile or log pile, for example. How many minibeasts visit your habitat? Can you identify them? Can you think of ways to attract more visitors?

What are we learning?

Small animals such as spiders, snails, slugs, worms and beetles are called minibeasts. They are invertebrates, meaning they don't have a backbone. The natural environment where you'd find a plant or animal is called a habitat. Minibeasts can be found in a variety of different habitats. Entomologists are scientists who study insects.

How to do it

1. We are going on a minibeast hunt to find out which habitats minibeasts like to live in.

2. Before we set off, sketch a quick map of the different habitats in the area that we will be exploring. For example, is there a pond, bushes, a leaf pile, stones, soil, trees or concrete surfaces?

3. On our hunt, spend a couple of minutes searching for minibeasts in each different habitat. Take a closer look at one with your magnifying glass, using a paintbrush to scoop the minibeast into your yoghurt pot. Then release it back where you found it.

Optional: Create a tally chart of how many minibeasts you find in each habitat. Which habitats are most popular with each type of minibeast? Why do you think this is?

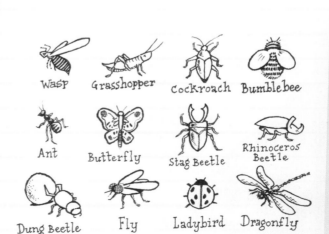

Wasp Grasshopper Cockroach Bumblebee

Ant Butterfly Stag Beetle Rhinoceros Beetle

Dung Beetle Fly Ladybird Dragonfly

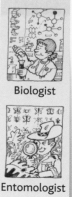

Biologist

Entomologist

19. MUSICAL MILK BOTTLES

Can we play a tune using glass bottles and water?

You will need

- Identically sized glass bottles x8 (e.g. milk bottles)
- Water
- A spoon
- A measuring jug
- Sticky notes (optional)

Investigate

Order the bottles from lowest to highest pitched. What do you notice? Ancient mathematicians like Pythagoras investigated the mathematics of musical scales. Can you find out more about this?

How to do it

1. The challenge is to play a tune without using a traditional musical instrument.

2. To produce a different pitch (sound frequency), each glass bottle should be filled with a different amount of water.

3. Measure out your water and experiment with making different sounds.

4. Perform a tune on your musical instrument. You can tap the bottles with the spoon or blow across the bottle tops. Discuss what you notice about the pitch of the sound and the volume of water in each bottle.

Optional: Older children could record the volume of water poured into each glass bottle on a sticky note.

What are we learning?

Tapping and blowing produce opposite results! When we blow across a bottle top we cause the air within it to vibrate, creating a sound. The more water in the bottle, the less space there is for air, so the air vibrates faster (making a higher pitch). With less water, there is more space for air, so the vibrations are slower (making a lower pitch). By contrast, tapping the bottle causes the glass to vibrate, rather than the air inside. This vibration produces a higher pitched sound when there is less water in the bottle.

Sound engineer

Mathematician

28

Can be done inside

Can be done individually

Suitable for teams

20. NEWSPAPER TOWERS

What is the tallest freestanding tower we can make out of newspaper?

You will need

- Newspaper
- Sticky tape
- Scissors
- A measuring tape
- A timer

Investigate

Research the tallest buildings in the world. What design similarities do you notice between them?

How to do it

1. Before you begin, quickly decide on a building strategy.

2. Start the 15-minute timer and set to work building your tower out of newspaper. Use sticky tape to join the structure together.

3. Check that your newspaper tower is freestanding. **Hint:** If it is not, remove some of the height and work on creating a solid foundation.

4. Time is up! Measure your tower to find out how tall it is.

Optional: Experiment with different designs and reflect on why some are more successful than others.

What are we learning?

A triangular or wide foundation will help to secure the structure. In real life, towers are often narrower at height as this helps them to better withstand wind. Your tower may have bent over because of its own weight. This is called buckling. Architects and civil engineers are often asked to create tall structures and have to make sure they are safe and strong. Just like in this task, they also have to deal with time and material limitations.

Architect

Civil engineer

21. OIL SPILL CLEAN-UP

How can we clean up after an environmental disaster?

You will need

- A 1-litre container
- Water
- Vegetable oil
- A teaspoon of cocoa powder
- Feathers
- Cotton wool balls
- A plastic cup
- A sponge
- A plastic spoon
- A timer

How to do it

Note: To minimise mess, wear appropriate clothing and conduct this activity outside.

1. Mix the water and oil in the container in a ratio of around 4:1. Mix in the cocoa powder and add the feathers.

2. There has been an environmental disaster! Imagine this container represents the sea after an oil spill and use the equipment provided to remove as much of the oil as possible into the plastic cup. You have 15 minutes. Each feather represents a marine animal that must be cleaned up.

3. Time is up! Measure how much oil is in the plastic cup, and how many feathers have been cleaned. How successful was the clean-up challenge?

Investigate

Use the internet to research how real-life oil spills such as the 2010 BP Deepwater Horizon oil spill have affected marine life. What could be done to help protect the environment in future?

Pelican

Sea Otter

Sea Turtle

What are we learning?

Oil spills can occur on water or land. A major cause is when the tankers or trucks that transport oil leak or have an accident. Oil spills have environmental consequences, particularly for marine life. The oil is poisonous to birds and animals and prevents their feathers or fur from repelling water and insulating against the cold. This is because the oil causes feathers and fur to mat and separate, exposing the skin to extremes in temperature. Oil also causes birds' wings to get too heavy, making it harder to fly.

Marine biologist

Environmental scientist

30

Best done outside

Can be done individually

22. PAPER PLANE BULLSEYE

What are the design characteristics of a successful paper plane?

You will need

- Paper
- Paper plane template (see page 32)
- A measuring tape
- Short- and long-range targets (e.g. cones)
- Scissors (optional)

Investigate

Research hang-gliding. How are people able to glide through the air without a motor? What forces are involved? Did you know thermal updrafts can keep gliders soaring for hours?

How to do it

1. Fold your paper to create a plane. Use the template sketches as a starting point. You can also try searching online for other designs.

2. Set out the cones you will use for target practice, placing your short-range one 5 metres away and your long-range one 10 metres away. Begin testing your plane with the short-range target. Can you get it to land near the target? Refine your design to make it land as close as possible.

3. Then create a new plane and aim for the long-range target. Spend time refining your plane to make it more accurate.

4. Look at the most successful designs for each target. Why did they work best? How do the short- and long-range designs differ?

What are we learning?

As we throw the plane we create thrust, a force that propels it forward. Real planes have engines to create thrust. Drag is a force working in the opposite direction and it is caused by air resistance (stationary air blocking the progress of the plane). The thrust has to be greater than the drag for the plane to advance forward. Gravity acts as a downward force on the plane. This is balanced for a time by the wings, which experience lift (an upward force) as the air passes over them. It is the balance of these forces that affects how far the plane will travel.

Aerospace engineer

Pilot

PAPER PLANE TEMPLATE

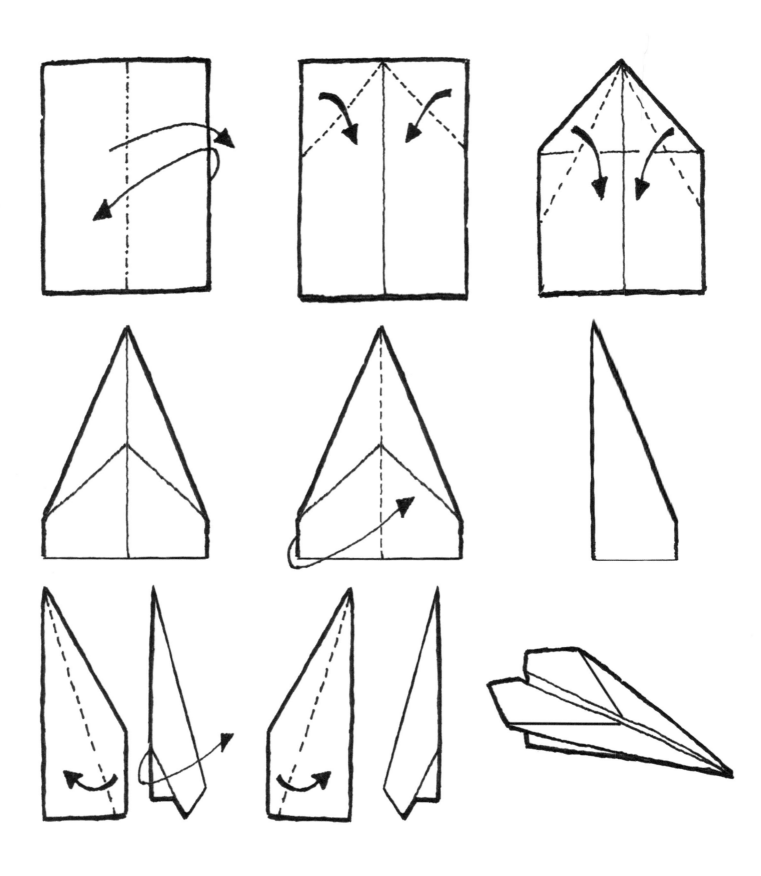

Resource from *15-Minute STEM* © Emily Hunt, 2018
Available to download from https://crownhouse.co.uk/featured/15-minute-stem

Can be done inside

Suitable for teams

23. PAPER CUP PHONES

How can we make our whispers heard a long distance away?

You will need

- Paper cups x2
- String
- A sharp pencil
- Scissors

How to do it

1. Take two paper cups and use a sharp pencil to make a small hole in the bottom of each.

2. Thread the string through the hole in the bottom of each cup, tying a knot inside the cup to secure it.

3. Now test your paper cup phone with a partner to see whether you can make sound travel between the cups. Keep the string taut.

4. Can you make sound travel around a doorway using your paper cup phone? Again, keep the string taut.

5. Now change the length of the string threaded between the two cups. How does this length change affect the sound?

Investigate

The discovery of how to convert sound waves into electrical signals was a major breakthrough. Alexander Graham Bell invented the first ever telephone. Find out more about his life and inventions.

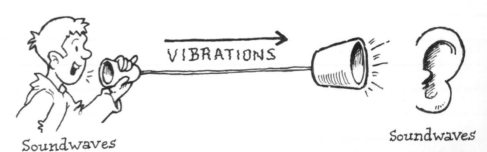

Soundwaves — VIBRATIONS — Soundwaves

What are we learning?

Sound travels through vibrations in the air. As we speak into one cup, the vibrations in the air make the cup and then the string vibrate as well. This vibration travels along the string into the other cup, which also vibrates. The sound created by the vibration is then amplified by the cup.

Some engineers need to understand how sound travels and is reflected by different surfaces. This is referred to as acoustics and is important in the design of some buildings (e.g. a concert hall, theatre or cinema).

Sound engineer

Electrician

Best done outside

Can be done individually

Suitable for teams

Be extra safety-conscious

24. PHOTO SCAVENGER HUNT

What shapes can we find in the natural environment?

You will need

- A camera, or phone/tablet with a camera
- Scavenger hunt list (see examples on page 35)
- A magnifying glass
- A timer

Investigate

Research some products that have been inspired by nature. How has nature inspired ways of making designs aerodynamic, waterproof or solar powered?

What are we learning?

The natural world is full of different colours, shapes and textures. The biological study of the shape of living things is called morphology. Engineers and scientists often take inspiration from nature when solving problems or designing new things. This is called biomimicry. For example, engineers designed the nose of the Japanese bullet train based on the beak of a kingfisher.

How to do it

1. Decide on the theme of your scavenger hunt. You could use one of the example scavenger hunt lists or create a new one linked to an area of learning or interest.

2. Take a copy of the scavenger hunt list.

3. You have 15 minutes to find and photograph an example of each item on the list. You must find natural rather than manufactured examples.

4. You can use your magnifying glass to investigate objects further.

5. When the time is up, review the findings and count how many items you photographed.

Optional: Make this into a competitive team challenge and see who can find the most items. Alternatively, try going to a different environment to see if you can beat your score.

Biologist

Mechanical engineer

SCAVENGER HUNT LISTS

TEXTURES SCAVENGER HUNT

- Spiky ☐
- Sticky ☐
- Slimy ☐
- Hard ☐
- Soft ☐
- Bumpy ☐
- Smooth ☐
- Rocky ☐
- Wet ☐
- Ridged ☐

2D SHAPES SCAVENGER HUNT

- Circle ☐
- Triangle ☐
- Oval ☐
- Square ☐
- Rectangle ☐
- Pentagon ☐
- Hexagon ☐
- Semi-circle ☐
- Diamond ☐
- Star ☐

PLANTS SCAVENGER HUNT

- Roots ☐
- Leaves ☐
- Pollen ☐
- Evergreen ☐
- Deciduous ☐
- Trunk ☐
- Seed ☐
- Soil ☐
- Petal ☐
- Fruit ☐

_____ SCAVENGER HUNT

- _____ ☐
- _____ ☐
- _____ ☐
- _____ ☐
- _____ ☐
- _____ ☐
- _____ ☐
- _____ ☐
- _____ ☐
- _____ ☐

25. PLAYING WITH PUDDLES

How long does it take for a puddle to evaporate?

You will need

- A cup
- Water
- Chalk
- A timer
- A measuring tape (optional)
- String (optional)

Investigate

Measure the perimeter (distance around the outside) of your puddle by placing string around the chalk outline. Then measure the string against the measuring tape. Which puddle evaporated the fastest, those with a bigger or smaller perimeter?

How to do it

Note: You will need to do this activity on a dry, sunny day to ensure the water evaporates. You will need to return to this activity throughout the day.

1. The challenge is to create a puddle that takes a long time to evaporate. Fill a cup with water. All of this water must be used to create a puddle.

2. Before creating the puddle, take some thinking time to decide on the best strategy. Will you pour all your water in one place or spread it more thinly over a larger area?

3. Create your puddle on a dry, flat surface in direct sunlight, such as the school playground or your driveway. Then draw around the outside of the puddle in chalk.

4. Begin the timer. Return to the puddle periodically to see how quickly it is evaporating. How long before it disappears?

Optional: Introduce a competitive group challenge, or repeat the experiment so you can compare results. Which puddle evaporated quickest? Why?

What are we learning?

Evaporation is a process that occurs when a liquid changes into a gas. On a warm, sunny day, air molecules move quickly with energy from sunlight, and water molecules in the puddle are warmed by the sun's heat. When energetic air molecules collide with water molecules on the puddle's surface, some water molecules receive enough energy to break free from the puddle, becoming water vapour. This reduces the amount of water in the puddle, so it shrinks. You will notice that a puddle with the smallest surface area takes the longest to evaporate. This is because there is less surface area exposed to the air.

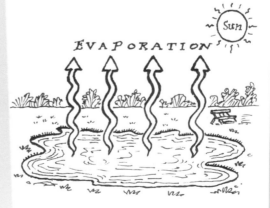

EVAPORATION

Mathematician

Meteorologist

26. PLUGGING PIPELINES

How can we transfer water across a distance without spilling it?

You will need

- Plastic cups x2
- A sharp pencil or compass
- Drinking straws
- Lolly sticks
- Masking tape
- A measuring tape (optional)
- Different sealants (optional)

Investigate

The Romans invented aqueducts to transport water into cities and towns. Find out more about aqueducts and Roman engineering.

What are we learning?

Liquids such as water and oil can be transported through pipelines in large quantities, as can gases. Sometimes this comes with risks, such as leaks. Environmental scientists assess the impact of pipelines on the environment, in their construction and operation. Considerations include the impact of an accidental release of a product from a pipeline, and how climate change could impact their function.

How to do it

Note: This activity could be messy so you may want to test it outside in case of spills.

1. You need to create a pipeline to transfer water from one cup to another without spilling it.

2. Create the pipeline out of straws, securing the joins with masking tape to prevent leaks. Make a hole in the bottom of one of the cups and attach your pipeline. You will need to use gravity to help the water move. This will involve elevating your pipeline and one of the cups using lolly sticks, so the water can flow into the second cup.

3. Time to test! Fill the elevated cup full of water and see how much reaches the second one.

Optional: The challenge is to make the pipeline longer without spilling the water (e.g. a 1-metre minimum length).

Optional: Investigate with different sealants to see which are best at preventing water from escaping.

Environmental scientist

Water engineer

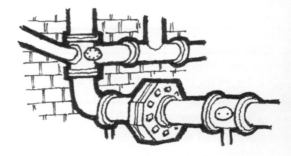

Best done outside **Can be done individually**

27. RACING HEARTS

How does our heart rate change with exercise?

You will need
- A timer

Investigate

How long do you think it will take for your heartbeat to return to its resting rate (the measurement you took pre-exercise)? Test this by taking several measurements and create a graph of your results.

Jogger   Runner   Sprinter

What are we learning?

Our hearts pump blood around our bodies through our arteries and veins. We can feel the blood pumping in arteries that are close to our skin, which allows us to measure our heart rate. Exercise causes the heart to pump faster. This is because working muscles need more oxygen to function, which is transported from the lungs via the bloodstream. People who do a lot of sport or exercise develop very strong hearts to deliver all the oxygen their muscles need. In order to keep our hearts strong we can exercise regularly and eat healthily.

How to do it

1. Begin by locating your pulse. Use the tips of your first two fingers (not your thumb) to press lightly on the inside of your wrist. Alternatively, press the same two fingers on your neck, in the hollow area just beside your windpipe.

2. Measure your resting heart rate by counting the beats for 1 minute. If you are impatient, try for 30 seconds and multiply by two! Record the number of beats.

3. Gently warm up by jogging on the spot for 30 seconds or jumping up and down ten times. Then measure your heart rate again and write it down.

4. Now think of an activity that will make your heart race, such as sprinting a short distance. Complete this exercise and then measure your heart rate.

Doctor

5. Now look back at your measurements. What happened to your heart rate when your level of exercise increased?

Statistician

Return to
activity later

Can be
done inside

Can be done
individually

28. RAINBOW WALKING WATER

How does water get from the roots of plants to the leaves?

You will need

- Clear glasses x3
- Water
- Food colouring (two primary colours)
- Paper towels
- Celery (optional)

Investigate

Now place a stick of celery in the coloured water for 10 minutes. Then cut up the celery and observe how the colour has travelled up the stem. This is an example of capillary action.

How to do it

Note: You will need to return to this activity throughout the day.

1. Place three glasses in a row and fill the two outer ones with water.

2. Place a drop of food colouring into one of the outer glasses, and a drop of a different colour in the other. Try using primary colours.

3. Take two paper towels and fold each one lengthways. Place one end of each towel in the coloured water and the other in the empty middle glass. Make sure the ends of the towels are touching in the empty glass.

4. Come back to observe the experiment throughout the day. Over time you will see the water 'walking' across the paper towels to create a rainbow of colours!

What are we learning?

When two primary colours mix together they create a secondary colour. This is what we see forming in the empty glass. The water travels up the paper towels by a process called capillary action. This is when water molecules join together and travel upwards through a material, thanks to the forces of cohesion (water molecules like to stay together) and adhesion (water molecules are attracted to and stick to other substances). In plants, water molecules travel upwards through narrow tubes called capillaries or xylem.

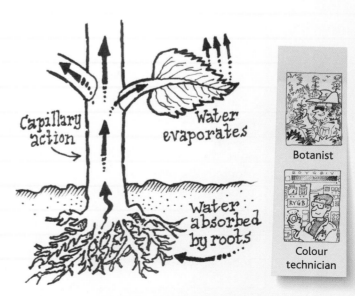

Capillary action

Water evaporates

Water absorbed by roots

Botanist

Colour technician

39

Can be
done inside

Suitable for
teams

29. ROBOT OBSTACLE COURSE

How are robots controlled?

You will need

- Chalk
- Hoops
- Cones
- String
- A blindfold

Investigate

If you have access to a floor robot (e.g. a Bee-Bot), have a go at directing this around your obstacle course. Is it easier or harder than directing a human? Alternatively, find out more about some of the jobs that robots are used for.

How to do it

1. Select one person to be the 'robot'. They will need to put on a blindfold.

2. Meanwhile, create a walk-through obstacle course for the robot using any of the equipment provided. It should have a clear start and finish point.

3. Then it is time to direct the robot around the obstacle course! Use clear, simple language such as, 'Take three steps forward. Turn right.'

4. Reflect on the activity: did the robot successfully navigate the course? If not, what could you do to improve?

Optional: Experiment by introducing more obstacles to make the course trickier.

What are we learning?

Robots are machines that can be designed with a certain amount of 'artificial intelligence'. Once a robot has been built, the final step is to program it. This program is a sequence of instructions, telling the robot how it should respond to its surrounding environment, and to the different situations it may find itself in. Each instruction must be clear and simple, so the robot knows what to do.

Computer
programmer

Robotics
engineer

30. ROCK RUMMAGE

In how many different ways can we organise a selection of rocks?

You will need

- A bucket
- A magnifying glass
- Sticky notes
- A camera

Investigate

Find out more about the human uses for different types of rock. In buildings, which are used for roofs? Which are used for walls? Which properties make them suitable for the different purposes?

What are we learning?

In geology, rocks are classified as igneous, sedimentary or metamorphic. Igneous rocks are formed when magma (molten rock) cools and hardens. Sedimentary rocks are formed when accumulated particles of material (sediment) are pressured together in layers over time. Metamorphic rocks are formed under the surface of the earth when other types of rock are subject to intense heat and pressure (metamorphism means 'to change form').

How to do it

1. Begin by going on a nature walk to collect several different types of rock in your bucket. They must be small and easily transportable, and you should not disturb plants or animals when collecting them. Ensure you have a selection of different sizes, colours, shapes and textures.

2. How could you sort your rocks? For example, from smallest to largest, or according to colour or shape. Add a sticky note to explain your chosen categories and take a photo.

3. Then sort your rocks again using different criteria. How many ways can you find to organise them?

Optional: As an extension, you could identify different types of rock using scientific terms (e.g. igneous, sedimentary and metamorphic, or permeable and impermeable).

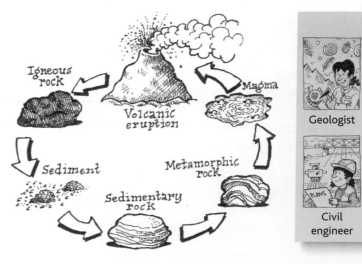

Igneous rock — Volcanic eruption — Magma — Metamorphic rock — Sedimentary rock — Sediment

Geologist

Civil engineer

Can be done inside

Can be done individually

Suitable for teams

31. ROCKET RACERS

How does a rocket launch into space?

You will need

- Balloons (different sizes)
- Thin string
- Plastic straws
- Sticky tape
- A timer
- Scissors

How to do it

1. Each racer will need a length of string, a straw and a balloon to make their rocket. Thread the string through the straw and tie it horizontally across the room (e.g. between two chairs). Arrange the strings in parallel lines and make sure they are equal lengths for a fair race!

2. Inflate the balloon and pinch the end to prevent the air escaping. Don't let go until the race begins!

3. Tape the balloon to the straw, with the end pointing away from the direction of travel.

4. Line up each rocket on one side of the strings and release them together, watching them fly along the length of the string. Time which rocket gets to the other end quickest.

Investigate

Now try experimenting with different-sized balloons or by adding more or less air. Alternatively, angle the string upwards or downwards slightly. What do you notice?

What are we learning?

When we blow up the balloon, we fill it with particles of gas. They bounce around inside the balloon, creating pressure. When we release the air from the balloon it exits quickly, creating a forward motion called thrust. In a real rocket the engines create huge amounts of thrust from burning rocket fuel, ejecting gases to propel the rocket into space.

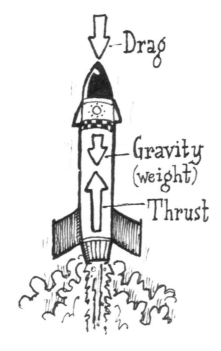

Drag
Gravity (weight)
Thrust

Astronaut

Aerospace engineer

32. SHAPE STRENGTH

What shape should we make a column so it will hold the most weight?

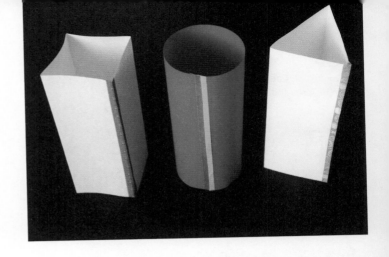

You will need

- A4 paper
- Sticky tape
- A pile of books

How to do it

1. Begin by folding A4 paper into three columns with different shaped bases: square, triangular and circular. Use sticky tape to hold each column together.

2. Which column do you think will hold the greatest weight? Why?

3. Test one of the columns by slowly stacking books on top of it. Count how many books it can hold before it collapses.

4. Repeat with the second and then third column.

5. Which shape held more books? Why do you think this was?

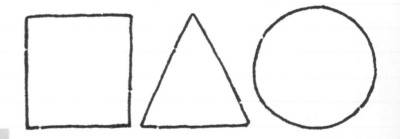

Investigate

How important is the size of the circle? Investigate whether changing the size of the column affects its capacity to hold more or less weight.

What are we learning?

The triangle and square designs shift the weight of the books to the corners of the column. This creates a point of high pressure which is too much for the paper. Engineers refer to this as buckling. Meanwhile, in the circle-based column, the weight is evenly distributed across the shape. This means more weight can be added before buckling. Circle-based columns are commonly used by engineers to support the weight of buildings.

Civil engineer

Mathematician

Can be
done inside

Can be done
individually

33. SWEETIE SYMMETRY

What happens when we put sweets in warm water?

You will need

- Colourful sweets
- A white plate
- Warm water
- A cup

Investigate

Symmetry is a fundamental concept in mathematics. It is common in nature and is also used by architects when they design buildings. Go on a symmetry walk and see what you can find.

How to do it

1. Position different-coloured sweets in a symmetrical pattern around the outside of the plate.

2. Slowly pour warm water from the cup into the centre of the plate until the sweets are half-submerged.

3. Watch as the colours from the sweets run into the centre of the plate. What do you notice happening to the colours? Why do you think this is?

Colour technician

Mathematician

What are we learning?

The coating of food colouring and sugar on the sweets dissolves and diffuses in the warm water (meaning it mixes in and spreads out). Each colour creates a solution with slightly different properties (e.g. density). This initially creates a barrier that prevents the colours from mixing and keeps them in separate layers. Scientists call this water stratification.

44

34. SPECIAL SNOWFLAKES

How does the pattern of a snowflake affect the speed at which it falls?

You will need

- Squares of paper
- Scissors
- A mirror
- A timer

Investigate

Research the life of Wilson 'Snowflake' Bentley, one of the first people to photograph snowflakes. What did he describe snowflakes as?

How to do it

1. Begin by creating a unique and symmetrical snowflake using your paper and scissors. **Hint:** Fold the paper into halves, quarters or eighths and cut the design along the fold line. Use your mirror to check that the snowflake is symmetrical.

2. Drop your snowflake from a fixed height, and time how long it takes to reach the ground.

3. Now adapt your snowflake design to reduce its fall speed.

4. Test again from the same height, compare the times and discuss why some designs fall slower than others.

Optional: Now have a go at designing a snowflake that will fall to the ground faster than your previous designs.

What are we learning?

Snowflakes are formed in the clouds when water vapour freezes. Every snowflake has six sides, but each individual one is thought to be unique. This is because each snowflake takes a different path to the ground, encountering different temperatures and moisture levels. Meteorologists study the weather to predict snowfall.

Gravity pulls the snowflake to the ground while air resistance acts as a force in the opposite direction. The less surface area (more holes) your snowflake has, the less air resistance there is, causing the snowflake to fall faster.

Meteorologist

Physicist

35. SPINNING HELICOPTERS

How can we make a helicopter out of paper?

You will need

- Helicopter template (see page 47)
- Scissors
- Paper
- A pen or pencil
- Paper clips
- A timer (optional)

How to do it

1. Make a copy of the helicopter template. You will need to cut along the solid lines and fold along the dotted lines.

2. Fold A and B in opposite directions to make the helicopter blades.

3. Fold C and D into the middle so they overlap, and secure with a paper clip.

4. Test your helicopter by dropping it from a height. (Be careful if you stand on a chair or table to do this.) Observe how it spins.

5. Try adding more paper clips to see how the added weight changes the spin. How many paper clips can you add before it stops spinning?

Investigate

Find out more about how helicopters work. Explore the different ways in which helicopters and planes create lift.

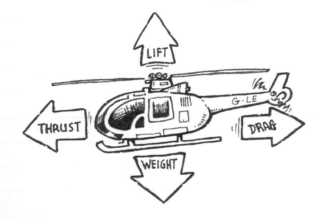

What are we learning?

Gravity is the force pulling the paper helicopter to the ground. As the helicopter drops, the air pushes up against the blades, causing them to rotate. In doing so they create lift, which helps to keep the helicopter in the air.

The direction the blades are bent in will affect whether it spins clockwise or anti-clockwise. Adding more weight will make the helicopter fall faster until eventually the downward gravitational force becomes much greater than the lift created by the rotation, causing the helicopter to fall straight to the ground without spinning.

Aerospace engineer

Physicist

HELICOPTER TEMPLATE

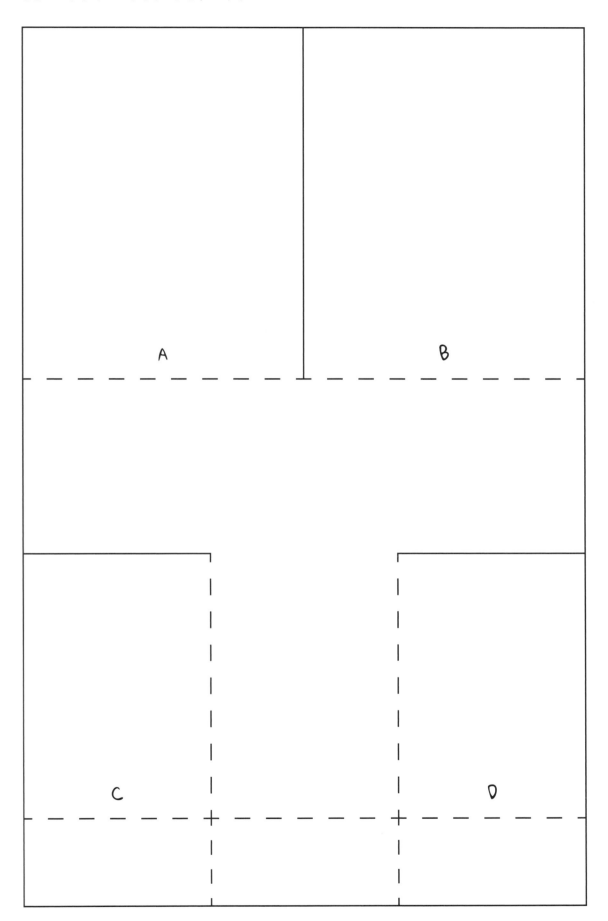

36. SPOON SOUND WAVES

How can we change the pitch of sound?

You will need

- Spoons (different sizes)
- String (approximately 2 metres in length)
- A ruler
- A fork (optional)

How to do it

1. Tie the middle of your string around the handle of your spoon.

2. Take each end of the string in a different hand, wrap it around your index finger and hold to your ear. The spoon should hang just below your waist.

3. Ask a friend to gently hit the spoon with a ruler.

4. Have a go at hitting the spoon with different amounts of force. Is it true that the harder you hit the spoon, the louder the sound?

5. Experiment with adjusting the string to different lengths. Does this change the sound?

Investigate

Try using different-sized spoons. Does this affect the sound? If so, why might this be? Does the sound change if we use a fork?

What are we learning?

When the ruler hits the spoon it causes the spoon to vibrate, creating sound waves. These sound waves travel up the string to your ear. Sound waves travel more quickly through solids, causing us to hear the sound more clearly. The string becomes a conductor for the sound waves.

Sound
engineer

Physicist

Can be done inside   Can be done individually

37. STATIC SALT 'N' PEPPER

How can we separate a mixture of salt and pepper?

You will need

- A tablespoon of table salt
- A tablespoon of pepper
- A plate
- A plastic spoon
- A balloon (optional)

Investigate

Find out more about static electricity. Did you know it can be used in devices like laser printers and photocopiers? Lightning is a sudden discharge of static electricity from clouds. Can you spot any lightning conductors on nearby buildings?

How to do it

1. Measure out one spoonful of salt and one spoonful of pepper onto a plate and mix the two together.

2. Rub the spoon against your clothing to create static electricity.

3. Hold the spoon above the salt and pepper to watch them separate! What do you notice?

4. Explore what happens when you move the spoon further away from the plate.

Optional: Use a balloon to generate static electricity.

What are we learning?

When we rub the spoon against our clothing we create static electricity on the surface of the plastic. The uncharged particles of salt and pepper are attracted to the charged particles in the spoon. The pepper particles are picked up more easily than the salt ones. This is because they are lighter, so it takes less effort for them to overcome the force of gravity.

Electrician

Meteorologist

49

38. TINFOIL CARGO BOATS

What design of boat will hold the most cargo?

You will need

- Tinfoil
- Coins
- Water
- A bowl, container or sink
- A weighing scale (optional)

Investigate

Create smaller and larger tinfoil boats shaped like canoes, squares and rectangles. Explore how the different shapes and sizes affect the weight they can hold.

How to do it

1. Create the hull of your boat using tinfoil. Make sure that the boat is well-balanced, with no gaps or holes, and that it has a high rim to keep water out.

2. Fill your chosen container with water and test your boat to check that it floats and is watertight. Adapt your design if necessary.

3. Then slowly add your coins (these are your cargo), one at a time. Be sure to balance the load to prevent the boat from tipping. Stop when the water reaches the top of the hull.

4. Count up your coins. You could also weigh them for comparison. How much cargo did your boat hold? How could you improve your design to make it hold more?

What are we learning?

Archimedes was an ancient Greek scientist and mathematician. Archimedes' principle states that the upward force on the boat, known as the buoyancy, is equal to the weight of the water it displaces (pushes out of the way). Different shaped hulls will displace different amounts of water, and therefore experience different buoyancy forces. As you add weight, the gravitational force pulling the boat down will increase until it exceeds the buoyancy, causing the boat to sink.

ball: displaced water weight < ball weight
boat: displaced water weight > boat weight

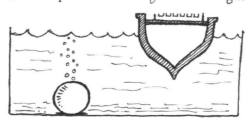

Sailor

Naval engineer

Can be done inside
Can be done individually

39. WATER COLOUR CARNIVAL

How can we turn primary colours into secondary colours?

You will need

- Large clear bowls
- Clear beakers
- A spoon
- Food colouring (primary colours)
- Water
- A mirror (optional)

Investigate

Now see if you can create a rainbow of colours using just a beaker of water, a mirror and some sunlight! **Hint:** Adjust the angle of the mirror above the water until you see a rainbow appear.

How to do it

1. Begin by filling a beaker with water and adding a few drops of red, yellow or blue food colouring. Stir to mix the water and colouring together.

2. Place the beaker in a larger clear bowl. Fill the bowl with water, making sure it doesn't overflow into the beaker. Add a different primary colour to the water in the bowl, stirring to mix.

3. Observe the two colours. You should notice that the light mixes to create a third colour.

4. Now try this experiment again with other colour combinations. How many different colours of the rainbow can you create using two colours? What happens if you use three?

What are we learning?

White light contains all the colours of the rainbow. As it passes through the first coloured solution, less of that colour light is absorbed, so that overall more of that light remains compared to the other colours. Then as it passes through the second coloured water solution, more of that colour part of the rainbow remains. So if we used yellow and blue colouring, the resulting light would have more yellow and blue parts of the rainbow. When this light meets your eye, the yellow and blue together are seen as green.

The primary colours are red, yellow and blue. When we mix them we can create orange, green and purple. These are called secondary colours.

Colour technician

Meteorologist

40. WATER FILTER CHALLENGE

How can we clean dirty water?

You will need

- A clear plastic cup
- Large and small stones
- Sand
- Cotton wool
- Muddy water
- A plastic bottle
- A timer
- Scissors

Investigate

Research the challenges involved in improving the water quality in developing countries. How can solar power help to filter water?

How to do it

Note: Do not drink the water, even when 'clean'!

1. Remove the cap and cut off the bottom of the bottle to create a funnel shape. Place the narrow end into the cup.

2. Line the bottom of the upturned bottle with cotton wool to act as a filter.

3. Fill the bottle with layers of natural materials, such as stones or sand. You could have a second go at this experiment, using different amounts of each material so you can compare how successful they are.

4. Pour in the muddy water, timing how long it takes for it to filter through into the plastic cup.

5. Visually compare the cleanliness of the water after each filter. Which materials were most effective at filtering the water?

What are we learning?

Tap water has passed through a water treatment system before it reaches our homes. This removes pollutants, making it safe to drink. Without this process, water may make us ill. Water engineers help to develop systems to clean water.

Clean water is not readily available in all parts of the world. Engineers and environmental scientists are working together to provide more access to clean water, particularly in developing countries.

Environmental scientist

Water engineer

STEM JOBS GLOSSARY

Aerospace engineer

Aerospace engineers design, build and maintain planes, spacecraft and satellites. They have to think carefully about how their designs will impact the environment. Aerospace engineers need to have good mathematical and problem solving skills.

Architect

Architects design buildings such as homes, schools and hospitals. As well as making buildings look nice, they also need to make sure that they are safe and serve the purpose they were designed for. They work closely with civil engineers to make sure designs are built correctly.

Astronaut

Astronauts go on missions into space, usually working as part of a crew on board a spacecraft. They are likely to need a degree in engineering, science or medicine. Astronaut selection is a tough process that includes physical, mental and academic tests.

Astronomer

Astronomy is the study of the universe beyond the earth, including stars and planets. Astronomers use telescopes and computers to observe distant phenomena, such as black holes or other planets. Their findings can help us to know more about how the universe works and about how it was formed over billions of years.

Biologist

Biologists study living things like animals and plants, which they call organisms. They consider how different organisms have adapted to their environment so that they can survive and successfully reproduce. Biologists specialise in different areas including zoology (the study of animals), botany (the study of plants), human biology and marine biology.

Botanist

Botany is the area of biology that studies plants. As well as identifying plants, botanists also help to conserve and protect them from pests, disease and climate change. Some botanists focus on studying plants that are used for food or medicine.

Chemist

Chemistry is the area of science concerned with how different sorts of atoms join together to form molecules, which are found in living systems (organic chemistry) or non-living systems (inorganic chemistry). Chemists use their knowledge of molecules and the properties of the substances they form to create and improve things like medical treatments and fuels. They often work in laboratories.

Civil engineer

Civil engineers design and oversee the construction of structures such as buildings, roads, railways and bridges. They also help to maintain them and ensure that they are safe to use.

Colour technician

Colour technicians design and produce colours in the form of dyes and pigments. These could be used in a range of things including dyes for textiles, ink for printers and paint for cars. A background in science or engineering is helpful in this career.

Computer programmer

Computer programmers create instructions for computers to follow. These instructions are called 'code'. They develop, test, maintain and debug (fix) computer programs. Many programmers have a degree in computer science, but it is a skill increasingly learnt by all scientists and engineers.

Dendrologist

Dendrology is a branch of science that specialises in the study of woody plants such as trees. Dendrologists know how to identify and categorise different trees. They work to protect woodland environments and spend a lot of time working outdoors.

Doctor

Doctors examine, diagnose and treat disease, illness and injury in human patients. Some doctors work as general practitioners in a local surgery, while others work in hospitals, which contain beds and more advanced equipment. A hospital is where people who need longer or more complex care go. Doctors often specialise in a particular area of medicine such as cardiology (the study of the heart) or neurology (the study of the brain and nervous system).

Electrician

Electricians install and maintain electrical systems, including lighting, security and fire safety systems. They work in a variety of buildings, such as homes, schools and factories and on new constructions. A high standard of training is needed to ensure they know how to work safely, as there are a lot of dangers involved with electricity.

Entomologist

Entomologists are biologists who study insects, such as ants, bees, butterflies and beetles. They are interested in their life cycles and behaviour and may observe them in their natural habitats. At other times entomologists collect insects and observe them in laboratories.

Environmental scientist

Environmental scientists study the impact of human activity on the environment. This includes areas such as air, soil and water pollution. They identify ways to minimise hazards and damage to the environment, such as by recycling packaging or using renewable energy.

Geologist

Geologists study the structure of the earth and its natural resources, and how they have changed over time. This involves analysing rocks, soil, fossils and minerals. They also assess the risk of natural hazards such as volcanoes and earthquakes.

Marine biologist

Marine biologists study life in the oceans. They are also interested in how human activities affect marine life and in exploring ways to minimise this impact. Many marine biologists spend a lot of time outdoors, including working on ships or diving underwater to monitor marine life.

Mathematician

Mathematicians either aim to understand the world using logic and abstract concepts (known as 'pure' mathematics) or to solve practical problems by analysing data with statistics and formulas (known as 'applied' mathematics). They often work closely with other experts, such as scientists or engineers, to solve problems.

Mechanical engineer

Mechanical engineers help to research, design, make and maintain a range of machines. These include spacecraft, aircraft, trains and cars. Mechanics is a branch of physics that deals with forces and motion. Mechanical engineers need to have a good understanding of this area to help them do their job.

Meteorologist

Meteorologists study and predict the weather. To do this they collect data about the atmosphere from weather stations and satellites. They use this data to make short-term weather predictions (e.g. it will rain tomorrow), and sometimes long-term climate predictions (e.g. the sea level will rise over the next 50 years).

Naturalist

Naturalists are scientists who study the natural world. In particular they observe how different species of plants and animals interact with one another in their natural habitats.

Naval engineer

Naval engineers design, construct and repair warships and other marine vessels such as ferries, submarines and yachts. They ensure that a ship's design is safe and strong.

Petroleum geologist

Petroleum geologists find and extract new sources of oil and natural gas, which is needed for heating, industry and transportation. This can be found both on land and at sea. They use technology including sonar devices and satellites to locate these sources.

Physicist

Physicists study the natural universe and use mathematics to explain how the world works. Physicists study different areas including space, atoms, sound and light. They can have wide-ranging careers as they are good at problem solving.

Pilot

Pilots fly planes carrying passengers and cargo on long- and short-haul flights. Larger planes are usually operated by at least two pilots, who take it in turns to fly. Pilots are responsible for the safe operation of the plane and need to be well-prepared and calm in an emergency.

Robotics engineer

Robotics engineers are responsible for designing, building and testing robots. Robots are machines with some degree of artificial intelligence, and can be programmed to perform jobs that are repetitive or too difficult for humans to do. Robots can be found in industries such as manufacturing, retail and agriculture (farming).

Sailor

Sailors work on passenger ships, tankers (which carry liquids and gases in bulk) and freighters (which carry goods). They have various jobs depending on the type of ship, such as safely stowing the ship's cargo, maintaining the ship, helping to navigate and steer the ship and ensuring it arrives safely at the destination.

Sound engineer

Sound engineers set up and operate sound equipment. They record and edit sound for a variety of media including films, video games, music concerts and sporting events. They are often involved in the development and application of new sound technology.

Statistician

Statisticians use numbers to understand problems and identify appropriate solutions. They find clear, visual ways to display information and make it easier to understand, such as using graphs. Sometimes they use statistical models to forecast what might happen in the future (e.g. to the economy or the climate). They need to have good mathematical skills.

Water engineer

Water engineers ensure that humans have a continuous supply of clean water. Their work may involve designing and maintaining water management systems to do jobs such as collecting water in reservoirs and storage tanks, disposing of sewage and preventing floods.

MORE IDEAS FOR NURTURING AN INTEREST IN STEM

I hope you've enjoyed the activities in this book and are now bursting with enthusiasm for STEM subjects! Here are a few final quick and easy ways to nurture children's interest in STEM.

- Encourage exploration. For example, a nature walk in the woods, a fossil hunt on the beach or stargazing on a clear evening.

- Take a trip to a local museum or zoo. This is a great way to not only bring learning to life but also to meet experts in different fields.

- Point out uses of STEM disciplines in our everyday lives. For example, calculating change in a shop or measuring ingredients for a cake. Help children to make connections between the skills they are learning and their real-world relevance.

- Find out how things work. Examples could include supporting children to take things (e.g. a simple mechanical toy) apart and reassemble them again. As you do so, discuss the role of all the different parts. (**Note:** Ensure that this is done safely.)

- Play puzzles and games. Puzzles and games, such as sudoku and chess, are great for developing logical thinking, an important skill in STEM subjects. Construction toys such as Lego help to develop spatial awareness. Anything involving dice is great for developing mathematical skills.

- Read STEM picture books. There's a whole host of books available that inspire interest and challenge stereotypes in STEM. See my website, How to STEM, for ideas.[1]

- Download STEM apps. From coding to virtual reality, there are lots of great STEM apps available, many of which are completely free. Again, there are plenty of ideas on my website.[2]

- Share your successes. Why not share your experiment results on social media using the hashtag #15MinuteSTEM? You could use Twitter, for example, to compare results and share ideas with other STEM enthusiasts.

- And most importantly …

- Be enthusiastic! Parents and teachers are important influencers of young people.[3] Keep your mind open to your learners' interests and be careful not to pass on any negative perceptions or stereotypes.

---

1 http://howtostem.co.uk/books/.
2 http://howtostem.co.uk/apps/.
3 Rhys Morgan, Chris Kirby and Aleksandra Stamenkovic, *The UK STEM Education Landscape: A Report for the Lloyd's Register Foundation from the Royal Academy of Engineering Education and Skills Committee* (London: Royal Academy of Engineering, 2016). Available at: https://www.raeng.org.uk/publications/reports/uk-stem-education-landscape.

FURTHER READING FOR ADULTS

Here are some of the books that inspired me to write *15-Minute STEM*. Although not exclusively about STEM education, they share a focus on developing real-world learning and equipping children with the 'future skills' they will need.

Boaler, Jo (2016). *Mathematical Mindsets: Unleashing Students' Potential through Creative Math, Inspiring Messages and Innovative Teaching* (San Francisco, CA: Jossey-Bass).

Boaler, Jo (2015). *The Elephant in the Classroom: Helping Children Learn and Love Maths* (London: Souvenir Press).

Claxton, Guy (2008). *What's the Point of School? Rediscovering the Heart of Education* (Oxford: Oneworld Publications).

Claxton, Guy and Lucas, Bill (2015). *Educating Ruby: What Our Children Really Need to Learn* (Carmarthen: Crown House Publishing).

Dweck, Carol (2017). *Mindset: Changing the Way You Think to Fulfil Your Potential* (London: Robinson).

Gerver, Richard (2014). *Creating Tomorrow's Schools Today: Education – Our Children – Their Futures*, 2nd edn (London: Bloomsbury).

Robinson, Ken and Aronica, Lou (2016). *Creative Schools: The Grassroots Revolution That's Transforming Education* (London: Penguin).

First published by
Crown House Publishing
Crown Buildings, Bancyfelin, Carmarthen, Wales, SA33 5ND, UK
www.crownhouse.co.uk

and

Crown House Publishing Company LLC
PO Box 2223, Williston, VT 05495, USA
www.crownhousepublishing.com

British Library of Cataloguing-in-Publication Data

A catalogue entry for this book is
available from the British Library.

Print ISBN 978-178583335-9
Mobi ISBN 978-178583362-5
ePub ISBN 978-178583363-2
ePDF ISBN 978-178583364-9

LCCN 2018951865

Printed and bound in the UK by
Charlesworth Press, Wakefield, West Yorkshire

Emily Hunt

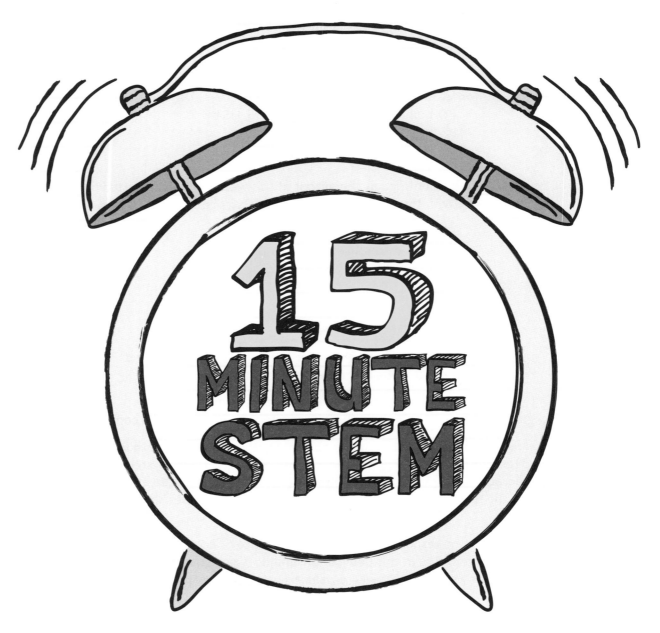

Quick, creative Science, Technology,
Engineering and Mathematics
activities for 5-11-year-olds

Crown House Publishing Limited
www.crownhouse.co.uk

15-Minute STEM is an inspiration. Its 40 hands-on activities are well-structured and, more importantly, intriguing. They are designed to capture the imagination, and succeed in doing so – my particular favourites are the Catapult Challenge and Rocket Racers (although this may simply reflect my desire to send things hurtling across a random space). The 'What are we learning?' sections in each activity also allow teachers to make connections to the curriculum, and enable the learners to understand the ideas behind the activities.

The book itself has a serious purpose, too – which is to engage and educate children in STEM education. This intention is clearly articulated in the introduction, which serves as a guide to effective practice in STEM. Here the exhortation to start with a question, expose the children to the resources and allow them to lead the exploration mirrors current thinking on the importance of engaging children in learning with a real purpose, and trusting them to lead elements of their own work.

The STEM jobs glossary illuminates another key purpose of the book – introducing children to the huge range of potential routes that are open to those interested in solving problems and tackling challenges. Certainly, inspiring an initial interest in STEM in primary school may be one of the key ways by which we can ensure that we have people interested in such work in the future.

Paul Warwick, Senior Lecturer in Education, University of Cambridge

PRAISE FOR 15-MINUTE STEM

15-Minute STEM is brilliant! It is packed full of fun and exciting science- and engineering-based activities that will engage and inspire children, helping them to develop enquiring minds through practical application. With its clear illustrations and step-by-step instructions, the book is great for parents to use with children at home – as well as for teachers who want to introduce more practical activities in the classroom. Fantastic!

Lynda Mann, Head of Education Programmes, Royal Academy of Engineering

I love this book! *15-Minute STEM* is crammed full of engaging practical ideas that are quick to do yet also inspire longer-term engagement. It's equally suitable for teachers and parents – definitely one of the best resources I have read in a long while.

Professor Bill Lucas, co-author of *Educating Ruby* and *Thinking Like an Engineer*

15-Minute STEM is full of activities that can be used to enhance current learning and provide hooks to get children thinking about new concepts. The tasks excite both adults and children alike, and naturally lead learners to explore and discuss ideas at their own pace.

A real treasure trove of creative learning opportunities that you can dip into time and time again.

Gilly Tyree-Milner, Forest School/Outdoor/Nurture Lead Practitioner, Worsbrough Common Primary School

Complete with easy-to-use instructions, *15-Minute STEM* offers an impressive collection of imaginative, interactive activities which encourage children to question, deduce and hypothesise as they learn. The book's format is simple to follow, with photos provided to illustrate a range of engaging tasks, and each activity is introduced with a question that stimulates children's interest and curiosity in STEM.

Our pupils absolutely love it!

Jo Lancett, Head Teacher, Darton Primary School

15-Minute STEM is an inviting, teacher-friendly resource packed full of tried-and-tested activities to help develop children's STEM skills, and is well suited to the teacher who is less experienced in teaching STEM subjects.

Each activity is explained clearly and concisely, and the eye-catching icons tagged on to the activities make it easy to prepare the ideal learning environment for each task. The links to the variety of related jobs also provide children with a useful introduction to possible STEM careers.

A great resource for teachers who are taking their first steps in creating a STEM-rich classroom.

Tanya Shields, Primary STEM Lead, STEM Learning Ltd

15-Minute STEM is a fantastic handbook for anyone looking to cram STEM activities into a busy timetable. Each activity is presented using child-friendly language, along with pictures and easy-to-follow instructions, and is set out in such a way that children will be able to pick up the aim of the task quickly.

The book features dozens of STEM ideas I have never come across before, and I can instantly see how they would be applicable in any classroom – either as stand-alone nuggets or as part of existing schemes of work.

STEM-sational.

Ben Connor, Teacher, St Maxentius CE Primary School